My First Bosnian
Alphabets

Picture Book with English Translations

Published By: MyFirstPictureBook.com

A
a

Avion

Airplane

B
b

Brod

Ship

C c

Cvijet

Flower

Č č

Ključ

Key

Ć

ć

Čekić

Hammer

D
d

Drvo

Tree

Dž
dž

Džep

Pocket

Đ đ

Grožđe

Grapes

E
e

Sunce

Sun

F
f

Flaša

Bottle

G g

Snijeg

Snow

H
h

Hljeb

Bread

I i

Igla

Needle

J
j

Jabuka

Apple

K k

Kuća

House

L l

Lopta

Ball

Lj
lj

Kralj

King

M
m

Mačka

Cat

N
n

Noć

Night

Nj
nj

Konj

Horse

O o

Oblak

Cloud

P
p

Pas

Dog

R
r

Riba

Fish

S
s

Sapun

Soap

Š š

Šećer

Sugar

T t

Trava

Grass

U u

Uho

Ear

V v

Voda

Water

Z z

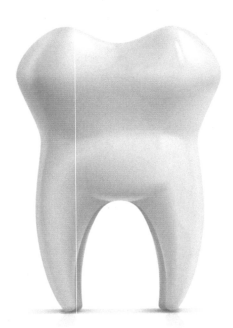

Zub

Tooth

Ž

ž

Nož

Knife

Made in the USA
Monee, IL
15 December 2021

85573419R00019